The Prince's

An Iraqi Folktale
Retold by Jacqueline Greene
Illustrated by Katya Krenina

Harcourt Achieve

Rigby • Saxon • Steck-Vaughn

www.HarcourtAchieve.com
1.800.531.5015

Prince Habib stopped weaving when his father entered the room. King Salim smiled at his son.

"You have become a fine carpet weaver and have learned a great skill," said the king. "You may be a rich prince, but always remember that it is important to learn how to do something well. A skill might help you one day."

Habib had heard his father's words a million times. The king thought it was very important to learn a skill. So Habib had learned how to make carpets when he was very young. It was hard work, but he liked to weave beautiful designs into the carpets.

"May I go out and ride my horse now, Father?" asked the prince.

"You have done as much work as ten men today," said King Salim. "You may ride, but do not go far from the palace."

Prince Habib prepared his horse for the ride. "If we ride fast, Pasha, we can go all the way to the mountains and still be back before dinner!"

The prince rode across the fields. Soon Habib reached the mountains, where there were tall trees all around him.

Suddenly a gang of thieves surrounded the prince. One thief held the prince's horse while another thief pulled the prince to the ground.

"Where did a small boy get such a fine horse?" asked one thief. "You must work for a rich man."

Prince Habib was afraid to tell the thieves that he was the son of King Salim.

"If we let him go, he might return and find our hiding place," said the leader with the black beard. "Let's tie him up. He will be a tasty meal for the forest animals."

Prince Habib was very afraid. He had to quickly think of a way to save his life. "I may be a small boy, but I am a good carpet weaver," he told the thieves. "I could make carpets for you to sell."

The leader thought for a moment. "Perhaps we should keep him alive," he decided.

The thieves pushed Prince Habib along a path until they came to a large cave.

The thieves tied the prince to a tree and gave him very little to eat for three days. Prince Habib worried that he would never see his father again.

At last, the thieves brought a weaving loom and some bags of wool to the cave. They untied Habib and said, "If you want to save your life, you must show us what you can do."

The prince worked very hard. All day and all night he pulled wool through the loom to create a carpet with a beautiful design. After a few weeks, the carpet was finished.

"This is the most beautiful carpet I have ever seen," the leader told the thieves. "We can either sell it in the market or sell it to a rich man."

"Neither one is right," said Habib. "If you take it to the palace and show it to the king, you will receive the best price for it."

So the leader rode off with the carpet.

Many hours passed, and at last the leader returned. "King Salim said that the carpet must be the work of the best carpet weaver in the land."

The leader tossed a bag of gold coins to the thieves, who fought over the money.

All of a sudden, King Salim rode up to the cave with his army.

"Habib!" cried the king. "I have found you! When the thief came to the palace with the carpet, I noticed that the beautiful design was a map. I saw a large crown and a vine leading to a cave. When I saw a small crown near the cave, I knew that you had made the carpet. I called my army and followed the map to find you here."

Prince Habib smiled. "Father, you said, 'A skill might help you one day,' and you were right. I learned to weave carpets, and this skill saved my life."